W9-BKV-745

DISCARD

Pebble™ Plus

Máquinas maravillosas/Mighty Machines

Portaaviones/Aircraft Carriers

por/by Matt Doeden

Traducción/Translation: Martín Luis Guzmán Ferrer, Ph.D.
Editor Consultor/Consulting Editor: Dra. Gail Saunders-Smith

Capstone press

Mankato, Minnesota

Pebble Plus is published by Capstone Press,
151 Good Counsel Drive, P.O. Box 669, Mankato, Minnesota 56002.
www.capstonepress.com

1 2 3 4 5 6 11 10 09 08 07 06

Library of Congress Cataloging-in-Publication Data
Doeden, Matt.
   [Aircraft carriers. Spanish & English]
   Portaaviones=Aircraft carriers/by Matt Doeden.
   p. cm.—(Pebble plus. Máquinas maravillosas=Pebble plus. Mighty machines)
   Includes index.
   ISBN-13: 978-0-7368-5864-9 (hardcover)
   ISBN-10: 0-7368-5864-4 (hardcover)
   1. Aircraft carriers—United States—Juvenile literature. I. Title. II. Series: Pebble plus. Máquinas maravillosas.
V874.3.A3718 2005
623.825'5—dc22   2005017946

Summary: Simple text and photographs present aircraft carriers, their parts, and their crew.

Editorial Credits
Martha E. H. Rustad, editor; Jenny Marks, bilingual editor; Eida del Risco, Spanish copy editor; Molly Nei,
   set designer; Kate Opseth and Ted Williams, book designers; Jo Miller, photo researcher; Scott Thoms,
   photo editor

Photo Credits
Corbis/The Military Picture Library/Clive Newton, 6–7; Peter Turnley, 8–9
DVIC/PH1 David Dentry, 1; PH2 Steve Enfield, 14–15; PH2(AW) Tim W. Tow, 16–17; PH3 Narina Larry, 18–19
Getty Images Inc./Phil Mislinski, 10–11; U.S. Navy, cover, 4–5
Navy Photo by PH2 Christopher Vickers, 20–21
Ted Carlson/Fotodynamics, 12–13

Note to Parents and Teachers

The Mighty Machines set supports national standards related to science, technology,
and society. This book describes and illustrates aircraft carriers. The images support
early readers in understanding the text. The repetition of words and phrases helps early
readers learn new words. This book also introduces early readers to subject-specific
vocabulary words, which are defined in the Glossary section. Early readers may need
assistance to read some words and to use the Table of Contents, Glossary, Internet Sites,
and Index sections of the book.

Table of Contents

Tabla de contenidos

What Are Aircraft Carriers?

Aircraft carriers are
the largest ships in the navy.
Some are longer than three
football fields.

¿Qué son los portaaviones?

Los portaaviones son
los barcos más grandes
de la marina. Algunos son
más largos que tres
campos de fútbol.

Aircraft carriers are
like floating airports.
Some carry as many
as 100 aircraft.

Los portaaviones son como
un aeropuerto flotante.
Algunos pueden llevar más
de 100 aviones.

Aircraft take off
from aircraft carriers.
They also land
on aircraft carriers.

Los aviones despegan
de los portaaviones.
También pueden aterrizar
en los portaaviones.

Parts of Aircraft Carriers

The main body
of an aircraft carrier
is called the hull.

Las partes de
los portaaviones

El cuerpo principal
del portaaviones
se llama el casco.

hull/casco

The flight deck is long
and flat. It looks like
an airport runway.

La cubierta para vuelos es
alargada y plana. Parece la
pista de aterrizaje
de un aeropuerto.

flight deck/cubierta para vuelos

The tower on an aircraft
carrier is called the island.
People in the island tell pilots
when to take off and land.

La torre en el portaaviones
se llama la isla. Las personas en
la isla les dicen a
los pilotos cuándo despegar
y cuándo aterrizar.

island/isla

The Crew

Thousands of people live and work on an aircraft carrier. They are called the crew.

La tripulación

Miles de personas viven y trabajan en un portaaviones. Son la tripulación.

17

Some crew members
fix aircraft.
Other crew members
fly aircraft.

Algunos miembros de
la tripulación reparan
los aviones. Otros miembros
de la tripulación vuelan
los aviones.

Mighty Machines

Tugboats help aircraft
carriers come into port.
Aircraft carriers
are mighty machines.

Máquinas maravillosas

Los barcos remolcadores ayudan
a los portaaviones a entrar
al puerto. Los portaaviones
son unas máquinas maravillosas.

Glossary

aircraft—a vehicle that can fly; airplanes and helicopters take off from aircraft carriers.

crew—a team of people who work together

flight deck—the long, flat area on top of an aircraft carrier where planes can take off and land

hull—the main body of a ship; the hull is made of layers of steel

island—a tower on an aircraft carrier that rises above the flight deck

navy—the military sea force of a country, including ships, aircraft, weapons, land bases, and people

port—a harbor where ships dock safely

Glosario

avión—vehículo que puede volar; los aviones y los helicópteros despegan de los portaaviones.

casco—cuerpo principal del barco; el casco está hecho de capas de acero.

cubierta para vuelos—área alargada y plana que se encuentra en la parte de arriba de un portaaviones donde los aviones pueden despegar o aterrizar

isla—torre del que se levanta sobre la cubierta de vuelos

marina—la fuerza naval de guerra de un país que incluye barcos, aviones, armamentos, bases navales y personas

puerto—muelle donde los barcos pueden atracar con seguridad

tripulación—grupo de personas que trabaja en equipo

Internet Sites

FactHound offers a safe, fun way to find Internet sites related to this book. All of the sites on FactHound have been researched by our staff.

Here's how:

1) Visit *www.facthound.com*

2) Type in this special code **073683656X** for age-appropriate sites. Or enter a search word related to this book for a more general search.

3) Click on the **FETCH IT** button.

FactHound will fetch the best sites for you!

Sitios de Internet

FactHound te ofrece una manera segura y divertida para encontrar sitios de Internet relacionados con este libro. Todos los sitios de FactHound han sido investigados por nuestro equipo. Es posible que los sitios no estén en español.

Así:

1) Ve a *www.facthound.com*

2) Teclea la clave especial **073683656X** para los sitios apropiados por edad. O teclea una palabra relacionada con este libro para una búsqueda más general.

3) Clic en el botón de **FETCH IT**.

¡FactHound buscará los mejores sitios para ti!

Index

Índice